Dearest Lynn
I thought this little
book would bring back
some wonderful memories
of Alfonso! We have "American Indian
Myths & Legends" to keep us
close ~ Love
Mom

Sandhill Cranes and Raven near Oxbow Bend, Grand Teton National Park, Wyoming

Soaring with Ravens

Visions of the Native American Landscape

Text and Photos by Tim Fitzharris

Foreword by Joseph Bruchac

HarperSanFrancisco

A Division of HarperCollins*Publishers*

Produced by Terrapin Books, Santa Fe, New Mexico.

First Edition

Library of Congress Cataloging-in-Publication Data

Fitzharris, Tim, 1948-
    Soaring with ravens : visions of the Native   American landscape / text and photos by Tim Fitzharris : Foreword by Joseph Bruchac.
        p.   cm. — (Spiritual journeys in nature)
      ISBN 0-06-251142-4
      1. Indian literatureTranslations into English. 2. American literature — Indian authors. 3. United States — Pictorial works.
    I. Title. II Series.
    PM197.E1F57   1994
    897—dc20   94-17099
                                                                    CIP

ISBN 0-06-251142-4

95 96 97 98 99   TER   10 9 8 7 6 5 4 3 2 1

Poppy Meadows, Tehachapi Mountains, California

For Nat

Books by Tim Fitzharris

The Adventure of Nature Photography

The Island

The Wild Prairie

Wildflowers of Canada (with Audrey Fraggalosch)

British Columbia Wild

Canada: A Natural History (with John Livingston)

Wild Birds of Canada

Forest: A National Audubon Society Book

The Audubon Society Guide to Nature Photography

Wild Wings: An Introduction to Birdwatching

Coastal Wildlife of British Columbia (with Bruce Obee)

The Sierra Club Guide to 35 mm Landscape Photography

The African Waterhole (with Audrey Fraggalosch)

Fields of Dreams

Sunrise, Grand Canyon, Arizona

Polar Bears, Hudson Bay, Manitoba

CONTENTS

Foreword

It begins with the earth. In the Wawenock story of how it all began, after Ktsi Nwaskw, the Great Mystery, made the world, there was still dust from that creation on the hands of the Creator. When that dust was brushed off and touched the earth, it shaped itself into the one we call Gluskabe. And when Gluskabe and the Creator climbed a hilltop to look around, they gazed wide-eyed in wonder at the beauty of creation on that first day.

That ancient tale from Wabonki, the Dawn Land of the Northeast where the sun first touches the continent of North America, is echoed again and again in the stories of Native people of this land. The earth gives us life. The world around is beautiful and meant to be viewed with respect and wonder. And when we see with a Native eye—whether our ancestry on this continent is as old as the first dust that fell on this soil or as recent as the vision of a new immigrant—we are touched by respect and wonder.

When we view the world around us in that way, we become aware of a spiritual connection which others may never experience. The Sioux holy man, Black Elk,

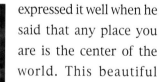

expressed it well when he said that any place you are is the center of the world. This beautiful

Chisos Mountains, Texas

Snowmass Wilderness, Colorado

creation is always speaking to us, it is just that we sometimes do not stop to look and listen. We forget to see as we

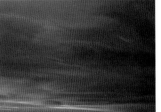

were meant to see, not just through our eyes but through the eye of the heart.

Twenty years ago with a group of friends, I climbed before dawn to a mountaintop in the Cascade Range in the state of Washington. As we sat there, waiting for the first light, a Lakota Indian man whom I'll just call Joe, came up to me and extended his hands. Held gently between his fingers was a meadowlark. "It came walking up to me," he said. "Birds like me to pick them up."

He placed the meadowlark in my hands. Then as I lifted it up and opened my palms, two things happened at the same time. The bright arc of the sun appeared to the east and, as the shadows ran across the wide green land, the meadowlark spread its wings and flew up, carrying our eyes with it into the dawn.

Joseph Bruchac

I

The Hunting Party

Southwestern Deserts
The Genesis of the Jicarilla World

In the beginning, everyone lived below the earth, for above was only water. Naturally, at such an elevation, it was dark and the people went about at half speed to reduce the effects of collisions and accidents, which were common. In the dim light sound was more important than today and so everything could talk—human beings, animals, trees and flowers, even rocks. You would hear, "Whoa, another step and you'll walk right off me and kill yourself!" if it was a red mesa, and if it was a buffalo, "Anything up ahead? I'm going to stampede." The prickly pear, however, had the same sense of humor as today's cactus, and it kept quiet.

Some people wanted more light. They had keen eyesight that was going to waste—the lizard and the pronghorn, or they liked to stretch out on a warm piece of ground to nap in the sunshine—the prairie dog and the fox. But the owl, the bear, and the

mountain lion, who made a good living in the darkness, wanted things to stay the way they were. They argued for a long time, and finally it was agreed to settle the issue by playing the thimble and button game.

The thimbles were made of wood, thinly carved wood that the lizard and the prong-

horn could see right through. They won every time because no matter where the button was hidden, they could see it. After the first round, the morning star appeared, scaring the black bear off to take cover inside a cave. After the second round, the edge of the world showed the first, faint trickles of violet energy, alarming the owl and sending him off without a sound into the dense foliage of a spruce tree. By the end of the fourth and last game, the round red edge of the sun had introduced itself in the eastern sky. The mountain lion flattened

White Sands, New Mexico

Yonder comes the dawn,
The universe grows green,
The road to the underworld
Is open! Yet now we live
Upward going, upward going!

Tewa

Turkey Vulture in Sonoran Desert, Arizona

South Rim of the Grand Canyon, Arizona

My words are tied in one
With the great mountains,
With the great rocks,
With the great trees
In one with my body
And my heart.

Yukots

into the grass, its tail beating back and forth. Then it ran off and hid in a canyon.

Conditions improved for most of the animals. The number of accidents declined, but it was still dim and living underground was depressing. On his travels, the sun noticed a hole through which he could see another world—the earth. The people soon learned about it and wanted to make the earth their new home. To bring them closer to the hole, they heaped up four mounds of dirt and planted them with flowers, fruit trees and bushes. The mounds grew into mountains and the seeds took root. Soon they were heavy with blossoms and berries where girls could gather fruit and pick flowers to put in their hair. Unfortunately the mountains were not high enough to allow the people to escape from the underworld. So they asked all of the eagles to contribute feathers that could be made into a ladder.

The feathers made a handsome ladder, but it sagged to the ground as soon as someone

7

8

*Everything as it moves, now and then,
here and there, makes stops. The bird as
it flies stops in one place to make its
nest, and in another to rest in its flight.
A man when he goes forth stops when
he wills. So the god has stopped. The
moon, the stars, the winds he has been
with. The trees, the animals, are all
where he has stopped, and the Indian
thinks of these places and sends his
prayers there to reach the place where
the god has stopped to win help and a
blessing.*

A Chief of the Oglala Sioux

Delicate Arch, Utah

climbed up on it. While the people were worrying over this problem, a buffalo wandered by and offered one of his horns (the right one) for the ladder. It made a perfect rung, straight and sturdy. Three of his friends came up then and contributed their horns. Soon the people were climbing up the ladder, through the hole, and onto the earth. They pulled the ladder up after them, untied the horns, now bent and curved from the weight of their steps, and gave them back. So a buffalo's horns are curved to this day.

The people sent the sun and moon up into the sky, tethered into place with spider webs. Tornado and some of his relatives were called to blow on the water that still spread over all the earth. They made four big storms that moved the water around and arranged it into oceans with dry land poking through. A black storm took care of the east, a blue storm the south, a multi-colored storm the north, and a yellow storm the west.

Everyone crowded at the exit of the hole like young billy owls, afraid of the strange world but stretching their necks this way and that for a better view. The storms had left a lot of mud everywhere and no one was in a hurry to get started on a new life. Finally a skunk and a badger set out together. They sank in the mud and returned with their feet stained forever black. Next out went the ferret. Soon his feet were black too, and he ran back in fright, splashing mud across his face and forgetting to lift his tail clear of the mess. He carries the same markings today.

10

Hole in the Wall, Death Valley, California

The beaver then tried his luck. There were still a lot of pools and running streams left over from the work of Tornado and the beaver, without a second thought, set himself to building a dam to store up drinking water for the people. The crowd at the hole still wasn't molified even when the beaver did not return. They sent out the gray crow to scout

the new territory. He didn't fly too far before he landed to feed on the fish, frogs, and snails that lay stranded and dying on the mud flats. The crow pecked at their eyes and swallowed their rotten flesh. This angered the people and they changed his color to black as punishment.

Finally, the people could wait no longer. Although they were still nervous, they gathered up all their belongings and started off. They headed east until they came to the end of the land, then south until the shores of the

13

Colorado River Canyon at Dead Horse Point, Utah

The Indian prefers the soft sound of the wind darting over the face of the pond, the smell of the wind itself cleansed by a midday rain, or scented with piñon pine. The air is precious to the red man, for all things share the same breath—the animals, the trees, the man.

Chief Seattle
Duwamish

Shiprock, New Mexico

southern ocean stopped them, then west, and then north with the same result. All along the journey different tribes dropped out of the caravan when they found a territory that suited them. By the time the huge circle was completed, the only people left were the Jicarilla

Apaches. They circled three more times until they angered the Great One who demanded to know their intentions. The Jicarilla explained that they wanted to live in the center of the earth. So he lead them to a spot near Taos where they made their home.

15

II

Otter on a Stormy Day

Rocky Mountains
The Flight of Caribou-footed

Naba Cha was one of the biggest men ever. He lived a long time ago near the Mackenzie River in northern Canada. A moosehide was needed to make each of his moccasins. For breakfast he ate a roasted caribou, and then another for supper. At night he could be seen in the light of the campfire smoking a pipe fashioned from the skull of a buffalo, scratching his hairy belly with fingernails like axe blades. His belches thundered down dark canyons, drowning the voices of wolf and owl. When he fell asleep, mice hunted in his hair for ticks and fleas, and skunks appeared from the darkness to eat the scraps of caribou meat strewn across his chest.

He went on the warpath often, traveling far in search of enemies. He fought the Eskimos on the shores of the Arctic Ocean and the Crees in the Great Plains to the south. Here he captured an orphan boy, named Caribou-footed, who became his slave and a target of his cruelty.

Each day Caribou-footed worked from dawn until past sundown, fetching water, gathering firewood, and cooking meals for the big man. If he slowed, Naba Cha lashed him

with a willow branch. And should he spill the water or fail to pluck every feather from the dozens of birds—grouse, ducks, and even eagles—that Naba Cha snacked on each day, the big man would rip out a clump of the orphan's hair between his thumb and forefinger.

But Caribou-footed had an ally, Hottah, a young moose, the wisest of the forest's animals. Hottah pledged to rescue his friend. One day while Naba Cha napped in the sun, he

18

Where the mountain crosses,
On top of the mountain,
I do not myself know where.
I wandered where my mind and my heart
  seemed to be lost.
I wandered away.

Papago

Eagle Flats and Tombstone Mountains, Yukon

Maroon Bells, Colorado Rockies

explained his plan to the boy. Hottah kept his words soft, letting them slip from his loose, furred lips with no more sound than a dove's wings, lest they wake the big man. "We will flee west into the land of Nesnabi, the Good Man, who will protect us. You must bring a stone, a chunk of earth, a piece of moss, and a tree branch." The young moose swung his head nervously around toward Naba Cha, but the big man snored, his jaw hanging open. "You will ride on my back and we will leave before tomorrow's dawn."

The first part of the journey carried them across the flat land west of the Mackenzie River. By the end of the day, they spotted Naba Cha following their trail, mounted on a huge caribou. Hottah told the boy to throw out the clod of earth, and immediately there arose behind them miles of rolling hills, and Naba Cha was lost from sight. The pair journeyed onward for many days, Caribou-footed eating berries and ptarmigan eggs, while Hottah paused often to kneel on the earth where his lips could reach the sweet grasses.

But one afternoon they saw Naba Cha again and Hottah ordered the boy to fling down the moss. Immediately a vast muskeg swamp formed behind them. They plodded steadily on toward the setting sun, while Naba Cha and the caribou sunk in the muck, floundering. A few days later, the big man appeared for a third time and Hottah instructed the boy, "Now throw out the stone." Caribou-footed lofted the stone into the air and when it struck the ground mountains rose from the earth. They soared upward, pushing through the

21

Moose in Snowstorm, Yellowstone, Wyoming

From Wakan Tanka, the Great Spirit, there came a great unifying life force that flowed through all things—the flowers of the plains, blowing winds, rocks, trees, birds, animals—and it was the same force that had been breathed into the first man. Thus all things were kindred, and were brought together by the same Great Mystery.

Kinship with all creatures of the earth, sky, and water was a real and active principle. In the animal and bird world there existed a brotherly feeling that kept the Lakota safe among them. And so close did some of the Lakotas come to their feathered and furred friends that in true brotherhood they spoke a common tongue. The animals had rights —the right of man's protection, the right to live, the right to multiply, the right to freedom, and the right to man's indebtedness—and in recognition of these rights, the Lakota never enslaved an animal, and spared all life that was not needed for food and clothing.

Chief Luther Standing Bear
Oglala Sioux

clouds, shaking out ice and snow that settled about their granite peaks. Thus the northern Rocky Mountains came to be, and their magnificent contours were visible for a hundred miles.

It took a long time for Naba Cha to find his way through the mountains, but eventually he was on the trail of the two fugitives again. Hottah asked for Caribou-footed to drop the tree branch and from it grew a thick forest of firs, spruces, pines, and tamaracks. Naba Cha was slowed and soon he was forced to leave behind the huge caribou whose sweeping horns had become lodged among the trunks.

By this time, Hottah had carried the boy to safety across a broad, cold river—the Yukon. Soon Naba Cha arrived at the river's edge, calling Hottah, asking for a ride across the rushing white waters, pledging not to

We were put here by the Creator and these were our rights as far as my memory to my grandfather. This was the food on which we live. My mother gathered berries; my father fished and killed the game. My strength is from the fish; my blood is from the fish, from the roots and the berries. I was put here by the Creator.

Chief Weninock
Yakima

24

Ponderosa Pine Forest, Arizona
Following pages / San Juan Mountains, Colorado

26

Stone Mountain, British Columbia

When the earth was made;
When the sky was made;
When my songs were first heard;
The holy mountain was standing
toward me with life.

Apache

harm Caribou-footed. It was while Hottah was stepping across the rocky river bed, his long

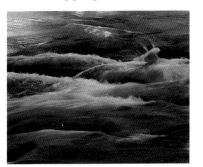

back bent beneath the giant's weight, that he pretended to stumble, his forelegs collapsing like a rotten ladder. Naba Cha was hurled into the icy water and was swept away, never to be seen again.

Thus, the landmarks were formed—the foothills, the miles of muskeg and black swamp, the singular evergreen forests, and towering over this landscape, which remains mostly empty even today, the northern ranges of the Rocky Mountains.

29

III

Sunshowers over Turtle Island

Eastern Forests
The Emergence of Turtle Island

A long time ago, before the earth came to be, there was nothing but an expanse of water. The only people were the animals that lived in the sea—waterfowl, seals, whales, and fishes. One day a woman fell through a hole in the sky. She plummeted downward, her body twisting slowly in the currents of wind, a godlike creature screaming out in fear.

Her cries were heard by a flock of geese who quickly signalled to one another to close ranks. They formed a large, flexible net of warm bodies that swooped beneath the woman, saving her life. The woman told the geese that her husband, Sky Holder, the chief deity of the heavens, had driven her away when he

North shore, Prince Edward Island

discovered she was pregnant. He had ripped up the tree of light and shoved her through the hole left by its roots. She beseeched the geese to save her child.

Immediately, the flock stirred with a hundred voices talking anxiously all at once, for only deep water waited below. The flock leader dropped back to fly beside her, "Fair woman, you can see that we are always on the wing or resting among the clouds. I must ask the other animals for help. They will find a solid place for you to stay." Then he stretched out

his black neck, and sounded the message to the world.

Eyes, ears, and noses began to appear on the water's surface as the animals gathered in council. A decision was made to send for the only being that could help them, and a muskrat was dispatched to the depths. Everyone waited while the geese circled above.

Soon a few bubbles broke the surface, fol-
lowed by a great surge and rushing and roil-
ing of the sea. Slowly the waters parted as a
broad, segmented dome covered with slime
and algae emerged. It grew larger and larger,
and finally the animals relaxed as Great Turtle floated into view.

"Place the woman on my back. It is the
only place where she can live," Great Turtle's
voice rolled over the waves and disappeared.
And so the geese set their wings into the wind
and delivered their charge to Great Turtle. It
was decided that the woman must have earth
for growing trees for shelter and corn for food.
So toad was sent to gather mud from the bot-

tom of the sea. He
surfaced a long time
later and everyone
gathered round to
peer into his wide
mouth. "Mud," they
nodded and con-
gratulated one another. Seal, otter, and muskrat began to spread the muck about the

*There is no quiet place in the
white man's cities. No place to
hear the unfurling of leaves in
the spring or the rustle of insects' wings. And what is there to
life if a man cannot hear the
lonely cry of the whippoorwill
or the argument of frogs around
the pool at night? Whatever befalls the earth befalls the sons of
the earth.*

Chief Seattle
Duwamish

34

Beech Forest, Adirondack Mountains, New York

Hornbuckle Valley, North Carolina

38

edges of the turtle's shell and soon there were forests, marshes, and meadows where the woman could raise her children.

She had twin brothers—one good, one evil. The good brother was born in the normal way, squeezing out headfirst from between his mother's legs. But the evil brother came into the world by kicking a hole in his mother's side and killing her. The boys grew like new grass after a fire, and within a month, they were mature and ready to make their mark on the world.

Good Brother let his eyes roam over the turtle's shell which stretched to all four corners of the horizon. "The world is empty. Let us fashion interesting creatures and fill it with life," and he sat down on his heels. Soon, a collection of bark, tree cones, lichens, mud, moss, and shed feathers lay piled at his feet. He began to assemble a menagerie of pleasant beings—a deer with a flashing white tail, a coyote that sang when it grew dark, a moose with round, firm muscles, and a beaver to make ponds and lakes for the fish people. He made butterflies that flew softly here and there, drawing nectar from flowers and filling the woods with flashes of color.

Evil Brother watched all of this closely, and when the butterflies appeared he began to manufacture his own insects. First he made mosquitoes with piercing noses for sucking blood, and then bees and hornets that droned noisily about he fields and stung the other animals. He created savage creatures with tough hides, claws, and narrow yellow eyes—bobcats, snakes, wolves, and grizzly bears—to terrorize the gentle, useful beings made by his brother.

Good Brother approached the giant

Shenandoah National Park, Virginia
Preceeding page / Lake of the Woods, Ontario

O our Mother the Earth, O our Father the Sky,
Your children are we, and with tired backs
We bring you gifts you love.
Then weave for us a garment of brightness:
May the warp be the white light of morning,
May the weft be the red light of evening,
May the fringes be the falling rain,
May the border be the standing rainbow.
Thus weave for us a garment of brightness.
That we may walk fittingly where birds sing,
That we may walk fittingly where grass is green,
O our Mother the Earth, O our Father the Sky.

Tewa

41

toad, sitting wide and pleasant in the sun. He crept into the shadows of the spreading belly beyond sight of the toad's keen eyes. Deftly, Good Brother sliced into the white skin. Toad blinked and a flood of water was released. It sooned formed beautiful rivers where a warrior could paddle his canoe without fear. But Evil Brother cast boulders into the currents to form rapids, carved the earth into waterfalls, and stirred the pools below to make them whirl dangerously. No matter what Good Brother did, it was rubbed out by the work of Evil Brother, and soon they resolved to fight one another for mastery of the world.

It was a strange weapon, a bag of corn. But with it , Evil Brother knocked his twin to the ground and pounded him mercilessly. He beat him until the body lay in the dust, a formless, bruised mound covered with ragged, bloody skin. Evil brother kept on until all life seemed to be gone from his brother. With his last breath, Good Brother called upon the spirit of his dead mother for help. Strength flowed back to his arms. He seized the antler

Father, paint the earth on me.
Father, paint the earth on me.
Father, paint the earth on me.
A nation I will make over.
A two-legged nation I will make holy.
Father, paint the earth on me.

Black Elk
Oglala Sioux

42

Lac des Montagnes, Quebec

Cove Forest, Great Smoky Mountains, North Carolina

of a deer and plunged it into Evil Brother, killing him. He stood over his dead brother, "From now on you will do good. You will be flint. People will use you for knives and tools." And so it was, but occasionally Evil Brother lapsed into his old ways, hurting people when they handled him carelessly.

The world was now big enough for the furred, feathered, and scaled creatures to reproduce on their own, and they scattered in four directions to live and die  naturally. Long after the creation of the earth, the forests, and the animals, Sky Holder decided that all was ready to receive the most beautiful creation of all—human beings. And he spread the Huron and Iroquois people over the earth.

For I have known you when your forests were mine; when they gave me my meat and my clothing. I have known you in your streams and rivers where your fish flashed and danced in the sun, where the waters said come, come and eat of my abundance. I have known you in the freedom of your winds. And my spirit, like the winds, once roamed your good lands.

Chief Dan George

45

IV

Love and Death at Sea

Pacific Coast
The Tricks of Raven

Numberless moons in the past, there was no earth. There was no existence outside of Cloudland, a kingdom ruled by Sha-lana. Below this was water—deep, gray, endless, and empty of life.

Sha-lana's chief servant was Raven, a black, shining presence with cunning ways. Raven's ambitious habits eventually angered Sha-lana and he was cast out of the cloud kingdom into the open space above the sea. Raven, happy at first with his freedom, wheeled about the heavens, sounding his pleasure. But when he grew tired and could find no resting place, desperation overcame him. He glided downward until his black knuckles trailed in the water, and began to beat his wings faster and faster. The seas

48

were whipped into foam that rose to a great height. Finally Raven became calm, and when the seas settled into place, they were changed into rock.

Waves worked at the rocks and in a few moons sand formed, and a few moons after that, the first trees sprouted. They grew quickly, stretching their limbs upward—spruces, hemlocks, red cedars, and pines. Raven perched on the uppermost branches, crooning in a bell-like voice about his creation. But soon he grew restless and lonely. He landed on the beach and gathered up an assortment of clam shells. He arranged them into two slim piles and soon after they were transformed into beautiful women. As you might expect, they soon complained to their creator about the absence of men. So Raven threw a limpet shell at one of them, taking away her breasts and giving her a penis. The man and woman mated and had

Boundary Bay, British Columbia

Del Norte Coast Redwoods, California

many children who became the ancestors of the Haida people, the first humans.

The happiness of the human beings caused Raven to return to Cloudland to find a wife of his own. He first transformed himself into a bear so that he would not be recognized by his old enemies. Cloudland had changed greatly in Raven's absence. Everyone was now a chief. Sha-lana had fixed a sun in the space overhead and it coaxed the animals out of hiding so that many of them spent a good part of each day laying about on the rocks, talking and watching their children play.

Raven stayed in Cloudland for several years, studying the new developments so that he could re-create them back on earth. One day he was stretched out on the beach in the manner of bears, his belly filled with clams and sea urchin gonads, his wide head resting on his paws. Except for the lack of a wife, he had been enjoying life. A disturbance opened his small, brown eyes and he viewed three young bears arguing over a red salmon. One bear would grab the fish in its jaws and bound through the shallows, while the others tried to snatch it away. Raven knew that these were the children of a great chief, who were, like himself, in disguise. He decided that this was the time to return home.

Using magic, he changed himself quickly into an eagle and stood at the water's edge, wings open to envelop the first gust of ocean air. Soon he was carried upward, yellow talons pressed into his body, eyes scanning the scene below. At a great height, he pulled his wings in, causing a stall that sent him into a steep

51

Big Sur, California

When I was ten years of age I looked
at the land and the rivers, the sky
above, and the animals around me
and could not fail to realize that they
were made by some great power. I was
so anxious to understand this power
that I questioned the trees and the
bushes. It seemed as though the flowers were staring at me, and I wanted
to ask them "Who made you?" I
looked at the moss-covered stones:
some of them seemed to have the fea-
tures of a man, but they could not an-
swer me. Then I had a dream, and in
my dream one of these small round
stones appeared to me and told me
that the maker of all was Wakan Tanka, and that in order to honor him I
must honor his works in nature.

Brave Buffalo

53

dive. The bears had no time to escape. Raven grabbed the smallest, and set a course for the sun which was disappearing behind distant hills. Dangling from the eagle's talons, the bear's screams echoed through Cloudland and word of the kidnapping soon reached his father, the great chief.

Of all the things in Cloudland, Raven was most fond of the sun and its soothing light. On earth, it was dark and there was always a lot of blundering and bumping into things. He was determined to return with this treasure. Meanwhile the people were rallying to save the chief's child. From above, Raven could see small heads of sea cows, otters, whales, and seals appearing one after another among the waves, and in the forest openings, the eyes of deer, muskrats, and wolves tracked his escape. Raven swooped low to pick up a firestick and lost his grasp on the child. It tumbled into the ocean where it was ferried to shore on top of a school of fish. Raven grabbed the sun under one wing, and dropped

54

By the sandy water I breathe the odor of the sea. From there the wind comes and blows over the world. By the sandy water I breathe the odor of the sea, From there the clouds come and the rain falls over the world.

Papago

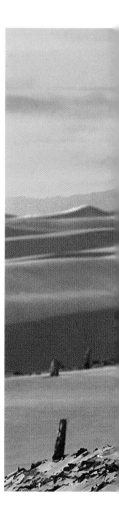

Coastal Sand Dunes, Oregon

to the ground beside the wall that protected Cloudland. He scratched out a hole and hopped through, taking the sun with him.

The earth appeared out of the darkness for the first time. Raven narrowed his eyes. He tilted and twisted his head. He stretched his neck, sighting through the hairs that sprouted from his bill. Then he took to the air, performing barrel rolls and somersaults. He swooped into the forests, brushing showers of dew from the shining leaves, but never touching a branch. He weaved unscathed through a maze of rocks that guarded the beach. He hung high on winds that played around the sharp corners of the granite sea stacks, greeting the puffins that nested on the ledges.

Still in good spirits, he began to tease the foxes that clambered along the cliffs hunting for puffin eggs. In a flash, one of the animals leaped, slim and limber, catching hold of the raven in its needle-like

Sometimes
I go about pitying myself
While I am carried by
The wind
Across the sky.

Chippewa Song

56

57

Long Beach, Vancouver Island

Leo Carillo Beach, California

Behold! A sacred voice is calling you!
All over the sky a sacred voice is calling!

Black Elk
Oglala Sioux

59

El Matador Beach, California

In the east is the dwelling of the sun.
On top of this dwelling place
The sun comes up and travels over
our heads.
Below we travel.
I raise my right hand to the sun
And then stroke my body
In the ceremonial manner.

Papago

teeth. In escaping, Raven dropped about half of the light from under his wing. It fell a long way onto the rocks, shattering into one large chunk and countless fragments that caromed off in every direction and disappeared into the sky. Raven was despondent over the loss. But later, when the sun had retired for the day, the light reappeared as the stars and moon, and Haida Gwai, as the kingdom was now called, grew more beautiful.

For a while after, Raven could be seen in the top of a hemlock, shaded by the tree's drooping frond, enjoying the view. He watched the human beings playing with the

firestick he had brought from Cloudland; he watched the whales hunting salmon and seabirds. But as was his nature, he soon grew bored with the lack of mischief in the world and set about the task of organizing some.

61

V

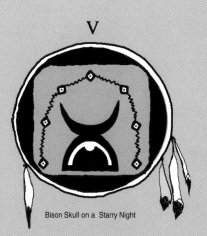

Bison Skull on a Starry Night

The Trials of Old Man Coyote

Once there was just Old Man Coyote living among the waters. Nobody is sure how he came to be; he just was and had been for a long time. Old Man Coyote was bored and lonely. One day he came upon two ducks—widgeons with blue bills. "Ah, little brothers," he said, "do you suppose there is anything around here besides water?" "Oh, yes," they replied, "there must be something in the deeps below."

At this, Old Man Coyote's ears stood up and he sat back on his haunches. "Well, little brothers, go and find it for me." Old Man Coyote waited while the wind blew through his whiskers, and the rain fell about his shoulders. After awhile his ears began to droop. But at length the ducks returned carrying a piece of root. "Oh, wonderful, wonderful," Old Man Coyote pronounced. "Where there are roots, there must be earth. Dive again, feathered brothers. Bring me some dirt." Soon the widgeons were back and

they placed a lump of mud at the coyote's feet. He sniffed at it and his long jaws opened in a grin. He blew on the lump and it spread far and wide forming a wide plain. Old Man Coyote was very happy. But the ducks implored, "Elder brother, make valleys for the rivers and hollows for the marshes. Make hills where the moon may hide. Make trees where we can sit and thick grasses to warm our eggs." So it was done, and Old Man Coyote was content once again.

But it wasn't long before he was restless, so he scraped up some mud and pushed and squeezed it into the shape of people. Old Man Coyote was excited and he strode about con-

Palo Duro Canyon, Texas

Pronghorn Antelopes near Manyberries, Alberta

I was born upon the prairie where the wind blew free and there was nothing to break the light of the sun. I was born where there were no enclosures and where everything drew a free breath.

I want to die there, and not within walls.

Ten Bears
Comanche

versing with these humans. But the widgeons complained. "Elder brother, you have created a wonderful place, but we need companions, too." Old Man Coyote stopped, one paw held above the ground as he thought. Finally he set it down. "Of course, you are right," and he went to work fashioning new animals—ducks in colorful variety, and buffaloes, antelopes, wapitis, bobcats, foxes, and weasels. And just when his younger brothers believed he was finished, he shut his eyes and made rattlesnakes, skunks, toads, and porcupines.

Some while later, Old Man Coyote was

stretched out on top of a mesa as the clouds and sun played together above him. All at once, Cirape, the coyote, appeared. "Why, younger brother, where have you come from?" Old Man Coyote asked, still

Shortgrass Prairie, North Dakota

Thunderstorm at Red Rock Lakes, Montana

My children, my children,
It is I who make the thunder
as I circle about—
The thunder as I circle about.
My children, my children,
It is I who make the loud
thunder as I circle about
The loud thunder as I circle
about.

Arapaho

sleepy. "I am just here. I exist. My name is Cirape, and what are you called?" "I am Old Man Coyote, and everything you see here I made."

Cirape looked around and he said, "Old Man Coyote, your people are poor. Give them travois and tipis. Give them bows and arrows to hunt buffalo and frighten their enemies. Give them war ponies to ride in battle." No one knows how, but Old Man Coyote did it, "The world is now complete." But Cirape exclaimed, "It makes me want to dance but there is no music."

Old Man Coyote folded his hands across his breast and cast his eyes upward. In a trice, a grouse appeared and began to play the tiny drum hidden within its chest. The music reached the antelopes on the plain below, causing them to race in great circles, flashing the white fur of their behinds. Old Man Coyote twitched a hairy ear and suddenly the sun rose and the mesa was covered with prairie

71

Moonlit Aspens near Milk River, Alberta

chickens. They tapped the ground with their tiny feet and waved their wings and sang into the wind. It was beautiful.

But a shadow fell across Old Man Coyote, still stretched out on the mesa, one foot dangling over the edge. It was the bear. "Old Man Coyote, these little birds should not be dancing. I am the one that dances. I shake the earth with my feet." Old  Man Coyote sat up, "But they are happy. Their bellies are full of gooseberries and rose hips. Yours is full of ice. You will not live among us. You will eat rotten meat and live alone in a cave and sleep most of the year so that we can be free of your darkness." And it became so.

One day Old Man Coyote and Cirape decided there was too much peace in the world. So Old Man Coyote gave tongues to the people—tongues that spoke different languages. The people became angry because they could not understand one another. The braves went on the warpath, stealing one another's ponies and making slaves of the young women. They counted coup and made gifts of their war prizes. Their great deeds were sung around the campfires during the long nights of snow.

Old Man Coyote asked Cirape, "If an enemy steals your wife, will you take her back?" "I have honor. I could not do it. It would be better if she were taken far away so my brothers would not think to laugh at my misfortune." "Oh, younger brother, you are ignorant. Three times my wife has been carried off on the back of an enemy's war pony, and always I

73

Everything was possessed of personality, only differing from us in form. Knowledge was inherent in all things. The world was a library and its books were the stones, leaves, grass, brooks, and the birds and animals that shared, alike with us, the storms and blessings of earth. We learned to do what only the student of nature ever learns, and that was to feel beauty. We never railed at the storms, the furious winds, and the biting frosts and snows. To do so intensified human futility, so whatever came we adjusted ourselves, by more effort and energy if necessary, but without complaint.

This appreciation enriched Lakota existence. Life was vivid and pulsing; nothing was casual and commonplace. The Indian lived—lived in every sense of the word—from his first to his last breath.

Chief Luther Standing Bear
Oglala Sioux

74

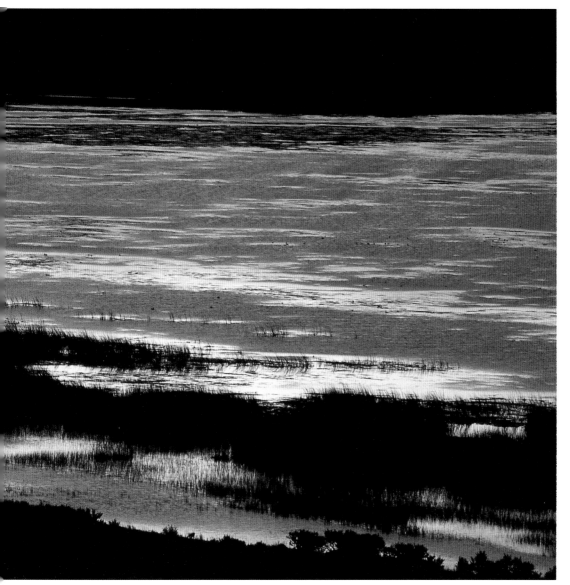

Last Mountain Lake, Saskatchewan

Near Black Coulee, Montana

have taken her back. So what if our brothers look at me sideways and laugh where my ears cannot hear. My wife knows she has been a slave, so now she is eager to please me. Each night under the buffalo robes she shows me the things she has learned in the camps of our enemies. The warriors may laugh, but tell me, Cirape, do our enemies steal the old and ugly, or do they take the young and pretty? There is nothing more satisfying than a wife who has been carried off once or twice."

The wise advice of Old Man Coyote was heard by the other people, and so it came to be that among the Crow, there is mutual wife stealing, and wives that have been stolen are taken back by their husbands. In one way or another, everything comes from Old Man Coyote.

Notes on the Photographs

The landscape photographs in this book were made with Canon 35 mm equipment on fine grained transparency films, mostly Kodachromes and Fujichromes. I used a variety of lenses varying in focal length from 18 mm to 500 mm. In most photographs, a polarizing filter and/or a variable neutral density filter were used to increase color saturation and control contrast.

The ravens which appear in the large plates were photographed in various locations of the southwestern United States. I took thousands of telephoto pictures of these birds in flight with the intention of sandwiching them with the landscape photographs. I chose the raven as a symbol of wilderness for several reasons. It is important in the culture of Native Americans, especially the tribes of the Pacific Northwest. Its habitation of wild and remote areas throughout North America (except for the deep south) allowed the book a nearly continental

scope. As a matter of photographic practicality, the raven's blackness makes it a perfect subject for sandwiching because the opaque image it forms prevents bleed-through of the underlying scenic image. The more I photographed ravens, the more I came to admire the obvious joy and beauty with which they fly and the apparent affability of their society.

When the time came to assemble the slides for publication, I decided to combine most of the ravens and landscapes using digital computer imaging techniques rather than making simple transparency sandwiches. This afforded much greater control over the process. My basic tools were a Macintosh Quadra 650, a Nikon film scanner, and Adobe Photoshop software. Once combined, the images were reverted to film for reproduction in this book.

Strangely, this technological advance has carried us back more than a century to a time when the visual documentation of events was charged to the painter. Photography's inception provided a way to circumvent the subjective views of the artist, and it became the preferred way of making visual records. Current technology erases the line that divides painting and photography. The camera becomes a sketch pad; a mouse or graphics tablet replaces the brush. The artist/photographer will embrace this technology. At the same time, this digital revolution suspends photography's unique, compelling, and ironic claim to art as document, and eliminates our trust in a means of communication premised on the objective transfer of information.

Notes on the Text

The tales in this book are drawn largely from Native American legends reported in the journals of European American historians and ethnographers. I have tried to retell them in the manner of the Indian oral tradition, allowing my experiences to intrude on the story, permitting the discourse to wander into territory I found pleasant and familiar.

Unlike Judao-Chris-

tian versions of creation, those of Native America are infused with humor. The North American wilds were evidently not spawned in sin and nurtured on righteousness and retribution. Underpinning the apparent glibness of these legends is a pervasive, sincere, natural, democratic, uncritical reverence for the natural world and the spiritual values of life.

Sources

Southwestern Deserts
Story based on an account by James Mooney. "The Jicarilla Genesis" *American Anthropologist II*, 1889, pp. 198-200.
Quotes
Page 3 Herbert J Spinden. *Songs of the Tewa.* Santa Fe, N.M.: Sunstone Press, ©1976, p. 93. Reprinted by permission. (Yonder comes the dawn . . .)
Page 7 Alfred L. Kroeber. *Handbook of the Indians of California.* Washington, D.C.: Bureau of American Ethnology, Bulletin 78, 1925, p. 511. (My words are tied in one . . .)
Page 8 Alice Cunningham Fletcher, "The Elk Mystery of Festival: Oglala Sioux" *Reports of the Peabody Museum, Volume III (1880-1886).* Cambridge: Salem Press 1887, Sixteenth Report (1882), p. 276. (Everything as it moves . . .)
Page 14 Chief Seattle, speech to the Governor, 1851. Washington, D.C. (The Indian prefers the soft sound . . .)

Rocky Mountains
Story based on two accounts: James M. Bell. *Fireside Stories of the Chippewyans, JAFL, XVI,* 1903, pp. 80-82. Ella E. Clark. "The Creation of Northern Rocky Mountains", Indian Legends of Canada. Toronto: McLelland & Stewart, 1960, pp. 99-101.

Quotes
Page 18 Frances Densmore. *Papago Music.* Washington: Bureau of American Ethnology Bulletins 90, 1929, p. 206. (Where the mountains crosses . . .)
Page 23 Luther Standing Bear. *Land of the Spotted Eagle,* © 1933, by Luther Standing Bear. Renewal copyright © 1960, by May Jones. Lincoln: University of Nebraska Press, 1978, p. 192-197. Reprinted by permission of the University of Nebraska Press. (From Wakan Tanka, the Great Spirit . . .)
Page 24 Proceedings of the New Jersey Historical Society, New Series, vol. 13, 1928, pp. 477-479. (We were put here by the Creator . . .)
Page 29 Pliny Earle Goddard. *The Masked Dancers of the Apache.* Holmes Anniversary Volume. Washington, D.C.: Government Printing, 1916, p.132. (When the earth was made . . .)

Eastern Forests
Story based on an account by Jay Miller, Ph. D. "Turtle: Earth Grasper", *Earthmaker.* New York: Putnam Publishing Group, 1992, pp. 44-50.
Quotes
Page 34 Chief Seattle, from speech to the Governor., 1851 Seattle: Washington State Historical Society. (There is no quiet place . . .)
Page 39 John G. Neihardt. *Black Elk Speaks.* Lincoln: University of Nebraska Press, © 1961, p.182. (Behold! a sacred voice is calling . . .)
Page 41 Herbert J. Spinden. *Songs of the Tewa.* Santa Fe, N.M.: Sunstone Press, © 1976 p. 94. Reprinted by permission. (O our Mother the Earth . . .)

Page 42 John G. Neihardt. *Black Elk Speaks.* Lincoln: University of Nebraska Press, © 1961, pp. 168-169. (Father, paint the earth on me . . .)
Page 45 T. C. Macluhan. *Touch the Earth: A Self-Portrait of Indian Existence.* New York: Promontory Press, 1971, p. 161. Reprinted by permission. (For I have known you . . .)

Pacific Coast
Story based on two accounts: Charles Hill-Tout. "Haida Stories and Beliefs" *Report of the 68th meeting of the British Association for the Advancement of Science,* 1898 (London, 1899), pp. 700-708. Bill Reid and Robert Bringhurst, *The Raven Steals the Light.* Vancouver: Douglas & McIntyre, 1984.
Quotes
Page 48 Daniel G. Brinton. "The Books of Chilam Balam." *Essays of the Americanist.* Philadelphia, 1890, p. 292. (Let us see, is this real . . .)
Page 53 Frances Densmore. *Teton Sioux Music.* Washington, D.C.: Bureau of American Ethnology Bulletin 61, 1918, pp. 207-208. (When I was ten years of age . . .)
Page 54 Frances Densmore. *Papago Music.* Washington, D.C.: Bureau of American Ethnology Bulletins 90, p.173. (By the sandy water . . .)
Page 56 Frances Densmore. *Chippewa Music I, II.* Washington, D.C.: Bureau of American Ethnology, Bulletins, 1910, 1913, p. 45, p. 53. (Sometimes I go about pitying myself . . .)
Page 59 John G. Neihardt. *Black Elk Speaks.* Lincoln: University of Nebraska Press, © 1961, p.182. (Behold! A sacred voice is calling . . .)
Page 61 Frances Densmore. *Papago Music.* Washington, D.C.: Bureau of American Ethnology Bulletins 90, 1929, p.137. (In the east is dwelling of the sun . . .)

Western Plains
Story based on an account by Richard Erdoes and Alfonso Ortiz. "Old Man Coyote Makes the World", *American Indian Myths and Legends.* New York: Pantheon Books, 1984, pp. 88-93.
Quotes
Page 67 T. C. Macluhan. *Touch the Earth: A Self-Portrait of Indian Existence.* New York: Promontory Press, 1971, pp. 147-148. Reprinted by permission. (I was born upon the prairie . . .)
Page 71 T. Mooney. *The Ghost Dance Religion and the Sioux Outbreak.* Washington, D.C.: Government Printing Office, Bureau of American Ethnology, 15th Annual Report , 1890, p.976. (My children, my children . . .)
Page 74 Luther Standing Bear. *Land of the Spotted Eagle,* © 1933, by Luther Standing Bear. Renewal copyright © 1960, by May Jones. Lincoln: University of Nebraska Press, 1978. Reprinted by permission of the University of Nebraska Press. (Everything was possessed of personality . . .)
Page 77 Luther Standing Bear. *Land of the Spotted Eagle,* © 1933, by Luther Standing Bear. Renewal copyright © 1960, by May Jones. Lincoln: University of Nebraska Press, 1978, p. xix. Reprinted by permission of the University of Nebraska Press. (We did not think of the great open plains . . .)

PRODUCED BY TERRAPIN BOOKS
Santa Fe, New Mexico